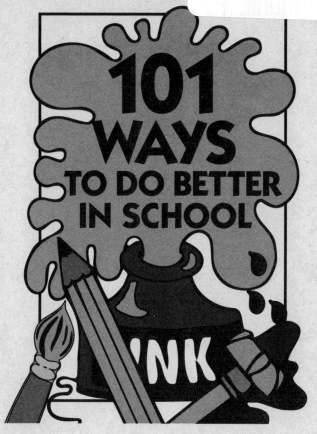

101 WAYS TO DO BETTER IN SCHOOL

Penny Colman
Illustrations by Paulette Bogan

Troll Associates

ACKNOWLEDGMENTS

Many of the tips and techniques in this book are from students themselves, teachers, and parents. A very special thanks to Ms. Patricia Zimmermann and the members of her 6th grade class, Smith School, Ramsey, New Jersey, who contributed wonderful ideas: Ryan Allen, Susan Braccini, Natalie Brier, Kyle Buffinton, Adam Butterfield, Erin Cadwalader, Megan Campbell, Tara Catanzariti, Jonathan Daffron, Jennifer Damiano, Kristiana DePaula, Joanna DeRosset, Carl Dietze, Geoffrey Dilly, Ian Dorman, Scott Doty, Dave Dunn, Jake Edinger, Emily Ferrara, Matt Franke, John Gormally, Laura Harvey, Robin Hauck, Liz Holl, Keith Lawson, Rob Lisi, Guy Malatino, Amar Mehta, David Murray, Mandar D. Muzumdar, Yuki Naruse, Ryan O'Connor, Andrew Ogden, Jennifer Oratio, Laura Ortiz, Simone Peart, Liz Pojanowski, Jeffrey Provost, Jessica Redin, Rhianna Richards, Brendan Robinson, Liana Rotolo, Shaida Safai, Brad Schwibner, Jillian Seibert, Jason Shanahan, Brad Siembieda, EJ Sobeck, Anthony Solarino, Mike Spies, Kristin Sternowski, Pam Vuijst, and Bart Webb.

Also thanks to Linda Hickson, Ph.D., Professor of Education, Teachers College, Columbia University, New York City, and Henry Oliver, Ed.D. Superintendent of Schools, Englewood, New Jersey. In addition, April Osborne provided helpful assistance.

Library of Congress Cataloging-in-Publication Data

Colman, Penny.
    101 ways to do better in school / by Penny Colman; illustrated by
Paulette Bogan.
       p.   cm.
    ISBN 0-8167-3285-X (pbk.)
    1. Study skills—Juvenile literature.   2. Self-management
(Psychology)—Juvenile literature.   3. Children—Time management—
Juvenile literature.   4. Homework—Juvenile literature.   [1. Study
skills.   2. Time management.   3. Homework.]   I. Bogan, Paulette,
ill.   II. Title.   III. Title: One hundred one ways to do better in
school.   IV. Title: One hundred and one ways to do better in school.
LB1049.C5814   1994
372.16'028'12—dc20   93-30872

A TROLL BOOK, published by Troll Associates.

Text and illustrations copyright © 1994 by Troll Associates.

Printed in the United States of America.

10 9 8 7 6 5

For April Osborne,
my daughter-in-law

Table of Contents

Table of Contents

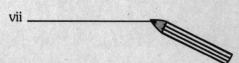

CHAPTER 1

Doing Better in School Pays Off!

Most kids don't really want to go to school. But, as everyone knows, you don't have a choice. There are laws. And there are parents. So, you go to school.

The pressure to do well in school is intense: Get top grades. Win awards. Be popular. Participate in sports and other activities. While excelling is easy for a few kids (or at least it seems that way), most kids find it tough. It's especially hard when teachers are mean, parents are unreasonable, classes are incomprehensible, and the other kids are snobby or nerdy.

So, why bother trying to do better in school? Because doing better in school pays off! Doing better in school makes it easier to win scholarships, to go to college, to get a good job. Doing better in school gives you more options and opportunities. Kids who do better in school please their parents and their teachers. And, most important, kids who do better in school please themselves! They feel more confident. More unafraid. More upbeat. More hopeful about the future.

Doing better in school makes sense. Good sense. And it's really not that hard. At least, it's not as hard as walking on the moon. Or hitting a game-winning home run. Or getting along with your family all the time. And it's definitely not as hard as getting gum out of your hair!

Best of all, you don't have to like school to do better. And you won't automatically become a nerd or a geek—unless you want to, of course. Kids who do better in school can be just as cool as they always were.

So, for those of you who want to succeed *and* remain cool, here are 101 ways for you to do better in school.

CHAPTER 2

Take Care of Yourself

1. Don't bug the older kids. You might end up with your head in a garbage can.

2. Eat well. That means you can't eat only chips, sweets, and fast food.

•It means a balanced diet with foods from the following food groups: bread, cereal, rice, and pasta group; vegetable group; fruit group; milk, yogurt, and cheese group; and meat, poultry, fish, dry beans, eggs, and nuts group. And not once a month, but every day!

•Soda and carbonated drinks have very little, if any, nutritional value. Fruit and vegetable juices do, so drink those. But watch out for "fruit drinks" that are mostly water, flavoring, and sugar.

The Food Guide Pyramid
A Guide to Daily Food Choices

Fats, Oils, & Sweets
USE SPARINGLY

These symbols show fats and added sugars in foods.

KEY ▲ Fat (naturally occurring and added)
◣ Sugars (added)

Milk, Yogurt, & Cheese Group
2-3 SERVINGS

Meat, Poultry, Fish, Dry Beans, Eggs, & Nuts Group
2-3 SERVINGS

Vegetable Group
3-5 SERVINGS

Fruit Group
2-4 SERVINGS

Bread, Cereal, Rice, & Pasta Group
6-11 SERVINGS

SOURCE: U.S. Department of Agriculture. U.S. Department of Health and Human Services.

INSTEAD OF EATING:	EAT:
ICE CREAM	ICE MILK and FROZEN YOGURT.
FRENCH FRIES	BAKED POTATOES.
CHIPS	POPCORN WITHOUT SALT AND BUTTER, RICE CAKES, and DRY ROASTED NUTS.
CANDY	FRESH FRUIT, DRIED FRUIT, and RAW VEGETABLES.
SODA, COFFEE, and TEA	FRUIT JUICES, NATURALLY FLAVORED SELTZER, and HERBAL TEA.

•Great snack foods include raw vegetables, raisins, nuts, rice cakes, popcorn, granola, and dried fruit.

•Studies show that kids do better in school when they eat a healthy breakfast. (Donuts and coffee are *not* healthy!) So, get up early enough to get a nutritious start.

3. Get enough sleep, but NOT in class.

•Different people need different amounts of sleep. Figure out the number of hours of sleep that you need to feel good and function well.

•Staying up all night to study or finish an assignment is a good way to end up walking into walls for a day or two. It's *not* a good way to do better in school.

4. Avoid alcohol, cigarettes, and drugs—the WARNINGS are for real!

•Alcohol makes depression worse. It also has a bad effect on a person's memory, speech, vision, judgment, and reflexes. Beer, wine, and hard liquor are equally harmful and can do permanent damage to a person's body.

•Cigarette smoke is linked to a long list of miserable and deadly diseases including lung cancer, bladder cancer, heart attacks, and strokes. Although some smokers insist that smoking isn't harmful and that they like the taste, the effects, and

16

the image, all the research shows that smoking comes with a high price tag—potentially deadly diseases for not only the smoker but for nonsmokers who inhale what the smoker exhales.

•Whether it's amphetamines, marijuana, cocaine, crack, or steroids, drugs will not help anyone do better in school! In fact, many drugs are quickly addictive and can cause serious and deadly physical and emotional damage. Drugs never helped anyone do better in school. Or in life.

5. Get plenty of exercise. Believe it or not, walking around the mall counts.

•According to studies, a brisk thirty-minute walk three to four times a week can increase physical fitness. And a physically fit person feels better and functions better.

•Use the stairs instead of elevators. Walk instead of driving short distances. Get up and turn the TV channel instead of using the remote control.

•While doing homework wiggle, stretch, and shimmy in your chair every 15 minutes. Get up and dance for 5 minutes every hour.

6. Make sure your eyes and ears are working okay. Ask an adult such as a parent or the school nurse for help if they aren't.

•Even if you don't have problems, a yearly physical check-up is a good idea.

7. Find friends who want to do better in school, too. Try studying together, but be careful! This will only work with friends who don't fool around too much.

8. Work out an agreement with your friends to limit the length of phone calls on school nights.

•An answering machine can be used to record messages until you're ready for a study break.

9. Find an adult who wants you to do well in school and who is willing to help. This may be a parent, but it doesn't have to be. Think of this person as your mentor.

•Talk with your mentor about how you want to improve in school. Be specific. For example, tell your mentor that you plan to get a "B" in science instead of a "C". Or that you're going to hand all your homework in on time. Ask your mentor for any suggestions about your plans.

•Give your mentor an update every week about your progress.

•If you have a problem that you can't handle, ask your mentor to help out. She or he could drive you to the library, talk to your teacher or principal, or loan you money for poster-board.

10. Seek help immediately if you have serious personal problems at home or with your peers.

- Many kids deal with a range of severe problems, including family members who abuse drugs and alcohol. And abuse kids. Families also cope with poverty and homelessness. It is very difficult to do better in school when things are terrible at home.

- Kids who don't have serious personal problems undoubtedly have friends and peers who do and need support and help. Be careful NOT to get in over your head trying to solve everyone's problems.

- Help can be found in many places, including your guidance counselor's office and the yellow pages of the phone book, which list agencies and organizations that help people.

11. Never cheat!

- You will lose the respect of other students.

- You will NOT feel good about yourself.

- You will risk getting into serious trouble.

12. Dress comfortably and in such a way that you feel good about yourself.

•It's hard to concentrate on doing better in school if you're worried about your appearance all day long. So, do your fussing at home and then forget about it.

•Dress to please yourself regardless of the current fashion. Remember, fads and fashions come and go. Besides, who's to say that your personal style might not catch on and set the standard?

CHAPTER 3

Pens, Paper, and Locker Combinations— Get Organized!

13. Select a wonderful workspace at home.

•This should be a spot where you feel happy and comfortable, but NOT sleepy. It could be a desk in your bedroom, the kitchen table, the living room couch, or a pile of pillows on the floor in the sunniest room in your house or apartment.

•Get a box or bag and fill it with all the study materials you might need: pencils and pencil sharpener, erasers, pens, notecards, paper clips, paper, dictionary, tape, glue, ruler, calculator, and different-colored pens for highlighting material.

•Write your name on the box or bag and a warning about what will happen to people who borrow stuff without asking you first. When you're not using the box or bag, store it in a special place such as under your bed or in your underwear drawer.

14. List a few reasonable goals for each marking period. For example, the grades you hope to earn, the study habits you plan to develop, the extracurricular activities you want to do, the books you want to read, etc.

•Pin the list up where you can routinely see it, perhaps by the bathroom mirror or on the television screen.

•Work out a plan for meeting each goal and write it in a notebook. For example, if your goal is to hand in all your homework on time, then your plan could include: not allowing yourself to make excuses such as forgetting to write down the assignment or leaving your book in your locker; not turning on the television until your homework is done. Give yourself a hug and a gold star for each goal that you accomplish.

15. Be sure to use dividers in your binder.

•Some teachers grade students for the neatness and organization of their binders. Don't blow this easy opportunity to get full credit.

CHECKLIST FOR STUDY SUPPLIES

_____ Dictionary

_____ Good light

_____ Notebooks

_____ Binders

_____ School books

_____ Assignment pad

_____ Schedule

_____ Pens with ink

_____ Pencils with sharp points

_____ Ruler

_____ Tape

_____ Stapler with staples

_____ Calculator

Other Supplies: _____

_____

_____

CHECKLIST FOR CLASS SUPPLIES

_____ Notebooks

_____ Binders

_____ Pens with ink

_____ Pencils with sharp points

_____ Erasers

_____ 3-hole punch

_____ Ruler

_____ Assignment pad

_____ Extra paper

_____ Calculator

Other Supplies:

_____

_____

_____

_____

_____

_____

MY GOALS TO DO BETTER IN SCHOOL
Marking Period

GOALS:	1	2	3	4
The grades I hope to earn:				
The study habits I plan to develop:				
The extracurricular activities I want to do:				
The community service projects I want to do:				
The books I want to read:				
Other interests I want to pursue:				

MY PLAN TO REACH MY GOALS

GOALS   **PLAN**

_____

_____

_____

_____

_____

_____

_____

_____

_____

_____

_____

_____

_____

_____

_____

_____

16. Keep all the papers and handouts you need in a place where you can always find them, and clean out unimportant papers once a week.

17. Avoid having loose papers. A 3-hole punch is a handy thing to have, so that you can punch holes in handouts, problem sheets, and graded tests and put them in your binder.

18. Memorize your locker combination so you can put your books away and get to your classes on time.

19. Don't just throw things in your locker. And if your locker or your binder starts to get messy, clean it!

20. Always carry extra sharpened pencils, pens, and note-book paper in your book bag.

21. Don't keep food in your locker more than one day.

22. Don't leave your gym clothes in your locker for over 30 days!

CHAPTER 4

Purple Pencils and a Reward— Get Motivated!

23. Get school supplies that are appealing and fun to work with, such as purple pencils, fat pens, and multi-colored paper clips.

24. If you hear yourself saying or EVEN THINKING that you're "stupid" or "dumb" or "lazy" or that "school is too hard," STOP YOURSELF! Imagine yourself throwing those words in the garbage or in a fast-flowing river that will carry them away from you.

25. Reward yourself! For example, call a friend when you finish reading a book chapter. Or make popcorn when you complete a set of math problems. Or after an hour of studying, go roller

skating. Or after finishing your social studies homework, read an article in your favorite magazine.

26. Think about doing schoolwork one step at a time. Instead of scaring yourself with the prospect of reading 10 pages or writing 5 pages or memorizing 30 things, remind yourself that you read one page at a time or write one page at a time or memorize one thing at a time. If that's too much, think about reading one paragraph at a time or writing one sentence at a time or memorizing just part of something.

27. If you feel yourself getting overwhelmed or discouraged, TAKE ACTION. Ask someone you trust for help—your parent, mentor, teacher, friend.

28. Make a list of why you want to do better in school. Keep the list handy and review it when you start to slack off.

29. When you complete an assignment, use a pen with your favorite color to check it off on your assignment pad.

30. Think about all the awful things you could be doing instead of going to school, such as walking across the Sahara Desert without any water or living in a country where the schools are closed because of a disaster such as war.

I WANT TO DO BETTER IN SCHOOL BECAUSE...

List YOUR reasons for wanting to do better in school. For example:

I'm tired of hearing my parents complain about my grades.
_____

I want to go to medical school.
_____

I want to join the honor society.
_____

I hate my purple wallpaper with red, green, and blue balloons, and I want to cover it with awards.
_____

_____

_____

_____

_____

_____

_____

_____

_____

_____

_____

_____

CHAPTER 5

Knowing What Makes Your Teachers Tick

31. Making fun of teachers will NOT get you a good grade.

32. Be thoughtful and considerate; don't give your teacher a hard time even if you think that she or he deserves it.

33. Follow all the rules that your teacher gives you.

•If you think the rules are ridiculous, politely ask the teacher to explain his or her reason for the rule.

•If you think the rules shouldn't apply to you or your class, write down your well-thought-through reasons and discuss them with the teacher.

•If you think the teacher was unfair to you, STAY CALM and prepare a case to explain your point of view. For example, you could get statements from other people who saw what happened. Discuss your perspective with the teacher. If other students are having the same trouble with the rules, organize a group and talk to the teacher together.

34. Listen to the teacher and make sure you understand what she or he is saying. If you don't, ask questions. If you still don't, arrange for extra help from the teacher. If you still don't, ask your mentor, parent, or a friend who does understand the material for help.

35. Never call out. Teachers hate it. Always raise your hand.

36. Don't interrupt the teacher.

37. Never talk back to teachers.

38. Be sure to understand the teacher's grading system. How much do quizzes, tests, homework, reports, class participation, group work, etc. count? Remember that every student is entitled to this information, so insist that the teacher provide it at the beginning of the school year.

•Also be sure to check whether or not the teacher marks off for neatness, missing headings, spelling and grammar mistakes in classes other than English, etc.

RECORD OF TEACHER'S GRADING SYSTEM

Teacher: _____

Class: _____

Homework counts for _____ %

Class participation counts for_____%

Quizzes count for _____%

Midterm exam counts for _____%

Final exam counts for _____%

Special project or research paper counts for _____%

The teacher gives extra credit. Yes____ No____

Other requirements include:

_____

_____

_____

_____

_____

_____

_____

_____

_____

•Also keep your own running record of your test grades and other graded work in case your teacher makes a mistake in his or her grade book. Keep your tests and other graded material for each marking period in a file folder. You can also chart your report-card grades to see where you are improving and what areas still need work.

•Check your progress with the teacher several times during the marking period. If the teacher says she or he is too busy, be persistent and come back again and again.

39. Figure out your teacher's pet peeve. Every teacher has one or more, as does everyone else, including kids. Once you know what the pet peeve is, avoid activating it!

Test Scores
(% Correct)

SAMPLE

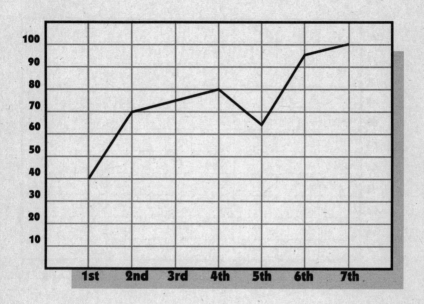

TEST SCORE PROGRESS TRACKING SHEET

Test Scores
(% Correct)

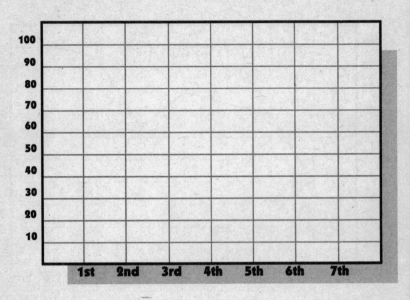

| | 1st | 2nd | 3rd | 4th | 5th | 6th | 7th |

TEST SCORE PROGRESS TRACKING SHEET

Grade Level _____ **Marking Period Dates** _____

Subject _____

Report Card
Grades

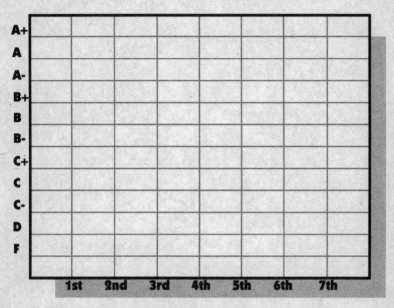

Marking Period

YEARLY REPORT CARD PROGRESS
TRACKING SHEET

Grade Level_____ Marking Period Dates_____

Subject _____

CHAPTER 6

Shining in Class

40. Go to the bathroom before class.

41. Don't fall asleep in class!

42. Always come to class prepared.

•With the right books.

•With completed homework.

•With 2 sharpened pencils and 2 pens with the right color ink.

•With the right binder and assignment pad.

•With any other supplies that are required for the class, such as a calculator for math, gym clothes for physical education, and an apron for cooking class.

43. Raise your hand. If you're not right, it's okay.

44. Always pay attention. The teacher calls on you when you least expect it.

45. During class discussions, pay attention to whoever is speaking.

46. When working in groups, let one person talk at a time.

47. Try to get along with the people you work with on group projects. Cooperation is usually part of the grade.

48. Never yell "Shut Up" at someone.

49. Think before you talk.

50. Don't fool around.

51. Don't throw spitballs.

52. Chewing gum in school is not smart.

53. Concentrate and do your best on everything.

CHAPTER 7

Getting the Most Out of Your Homework

54. Buy a dog so you can say it ate your homework when you don't have it.

55. Write assignments in your assigment pad right away before you forget them.

56. Make sure before you go home that you have everything you need.

57. Figure out the best time, place, and routines for doing your homework.

58. Take your work seriously. Let it represent the best you are and the best that you'd like to become.

ASSIGNMENT LOG

Dates: From _____ To _____

Subject Area	Assignment	Date Due	Estimate of Time Needed	Resources Needed	Completed

48

59. Take your time and do your assignment the right way.

60. Always check to see if you did all your homework.

61. Look for extra books, magazine articles, and newspaper stories about the topics and subjects that you are studying. When you find them, READ, READ, READ! Your brain can store TONS of information. So, fill it up and draw upon it when you need it!

62. Do not throw your homework in the garbage.

63. Do some of your homework in the public library. You may find interesting books, magazines, videos, tapes, and friends.

64. Get a big monthly calendar.

•Write in test dates.

•In different color ink, write in project and paper due dates.

•Block out MORE time than you will actually need for studying and homework each week. It's important to block out more time to allow for varying assignments and interruptions.

MONTHLY PLANNING CALENDAR

MONTH _____ **YEAR** _____

DATE	Monday	Tuesday	Wednesday	Thursday	Friday	Saturday	Sunday

•Before deciding to do an unanticipated activity that would cut into your study time, GO to your calendar and block out an equivalent amount of make-up time.

65. Use a daily schedule sheet to plan your day after school.

•List your homework assignments in the order in which you plan to do them.

•Estimate the time needed to complete each assignment.

•If you finish early, use the remaining time to do extra studying or reading.

•If you haven't allotted enough time to do your homework, then take the time out of another activity you planned to do that day such as playing ball or watching television or talking on the telephone.

DAILY HOMEWORK PLANNER

Schedule of Activities & Tasks   **Date** ___

TIME PERIOD	ACTIVITY/TASK	COMPLETED
3 - 3:30		
3:30 - 4		
4 - 4:30		
4:30 - 5		
5 - 5:30		
5:30 - 6		
6 - 6:30		
6:30 - 7		
7 - 7:30		
7:30 - 8		
8 - 8:30		
8:30 - 9		
9 - 9:30		
9:30 - 10		
10 - 10:30		
10:30 - 11		
11 - 11:30		

WEEKLY PLANNER
Priority Tasks

DATES	MONTH	YEAR
M O N		
T U E		
W E D		
T H U		
F R I		
S A T		
S U N		

CHAPTER 8

Succeeding at Studying and Test Taking

66. Study hard.

67. Set goals.

•Aim for a realistic amount of improvement each time you take a test.

68. Figure out what method of studying works best for you.

•Alone?

•With friends?

•With a study pal, who is not necessarily a friend, for specific assignments?

•Reviewing the material by talking out loud to yourself?

•Writing material over and over again?

•Having an adult quiz you?

•Using a tape recorder to record important information and then listening to it over and over again?

•Explaining the material in your own words so that your dog or cat or goldfish understands it?

•All of the above?

69. Use mnemonics, or memory aids, to help you remember things.

•Organize lists of things to remember into categories. For example, green foods and yellow foods.

•Make up a word with the first letters of terms to be remembered. For example, HOMES will help you remember the names of the Great Lakes—Huron, Ontario, Michigan, Erie, and Superior.

MNEMONIC OR MEMORY AIDS

Make up a word with the first letters of terms to be remembered. These are called acronyms and include:

*HOMES	*ROY G BIV	*FOIL
for the names of the Great Lakes	for the colors of the spectrum (or a rainbow when you see one)	for how to factor algebraic equations
HURON	**R**ED	**F**IRST
ONTARIO	**O**RANGE	**O**UTER
MICHIGAN	**Y**ELLOW	**I**NNER
ERIE	**G**REEN	**L**AST
SUPERIOR	**B**LUE	
	INDIGO	
	VIOLET	

•Make up a funny sentence with the first letters of terms to be remembered. For example, NO PLAN LIKE YOURS TO STUDY HISTORY WISELY helps you remember the royal houses of England, which are: Norman, Plantagenet, Lancaster, York, Tudor, Stuart, Hanover, and Windsor.

•Use visual images to help you remember sentences and stories. For example, the sentence "The ghost wore sunglasses" is easier to remember if you imagine a big, white ghost wearing green sunglasses.

•Remember numbers in groups of 3 or 4. For example, it is much easier to remember a phone number divided into chunks, such as (612) 568-8832, than the same number in an undivided string of ten numerals: 6125688832.

•Make up a rhyme such as the calendar rhyme that will help you remember the number of days in each month:

> Thirty days hath September
> April, June, and November.
> February 8 and 20 all alone.
> All the rest have 31,
> Unless that Leap Year doth combine
> And give to February 29.

70. While studying, keep asking yourself if you understand the material. If not, look up a word in the dictionary, reread what you didn't understand, or ask someone for help.

71. Seek help when you don't understand something. Never cover up what you don't know because it only gets worse.

72. Keep up with your schoolwork. Even if you don't have homework, do some reading or studying every day. Soon you'll begin to feel more confident.

73. Give yourself a break. Plan your studying so you can take time to watch your favorite television show or talk to a friend or play a game without feeling guilty.

74. When you get tests and assignments back, make sure you understand every mistake you made. If you don't know how to correct the mistake, ask for help.

75. Pretend that you're the teacher and think about what questions she or he would put on the test.

•Review your notes, reading assignments, and homework and underline or highlight the information the teacher stressed.

•Make sure that you thoroughly know the information that was important to the teacher.

•Make sure you know what type of test the teacher gives: multiple choice, true/false, essay questions, or a combination of the three.

76. Do sample problems and exercises.

•Start early and leave time to get help with the problems you can't solve.

77. Don't skip over sidebar articles or margin notes in the textbook. Teachers sometimes like to base a question on that information.

78. Quiz yourself.

79. If your teacher gives you a pre-test to do at home, DO IT!

80. Note the information that gives you the most trouble and review it right before the test.

81. Concentrate on your test and do not let anything bother you.

82. Plan your time during the test so that you have time to answer all of the questions.

83. Check your work after the test.

84. When the teacher returns your test, review it carefully. Double-check that the teacher didn't make a mistake in correcting multiple choice and true and false questions. Also reread your essays. If the teacher deducted points, make sure you understand why. If you don't agree with the teacher's assessment, carefully present your case and ask the teacher to reassess your essay.

A sidebar appears on a book page in addition to the regular text. It is a short article about a person, idea, or event. It usually has a different colored background than the regular text. It is also frequently outlined with a border and has different type than the regular text.

Margin notes are found in the white space beside the text. Sometimes they are in a box and have different type than the regular text or sidebar.

CHAPTER 9

Writing, Writing, and More Writing

85. To write better—READ, READ, READ.

•Ask someone you like to recommend a book that they read and liked. Discuss it together.

86. To write better—WRITE, WRITE, WRITE.

•Letters to friends, relatives, or to the newspaper.

•A record of your daily thoughts and activities.

•Rap lyrics.

•Jokes, advertising jingles, or love songs.

•A plot and dialogue for a television show or movie.

LISTS OF BOOKS I'VE READ

Title:
Author:
Publisher:
Publication date:
Type of book:
Number of pages:
My comments:

Title:
Author:
Publisher:
Publication date:
Type of book:
Number of pages:
My comments:

Title:
Author:
Publisher:
Publication date:
Type of book:
Number of pages:
My comments:

•Short stories.

•A campaign speech for a politician.

87. Find a computer at home, school, or the library that you can have access to on a regular basis.

•Take a class, buy an instruction book, or enlist a knowledge-able friend and learn a word processing program.

•Practice until you can sit down and write something with-out hesitation. It may take time, but it's worth it because word processing programs make it so easy to revise and edit your reports and papers.

88. While you're learning to use the computer, don't stop writing with a pen or pencil or typewriter. In fact, don't ever stop writing with a pen or pencil!

89. Always carry a pen and notebook that is small enough to fit in your pocket. Jot down interesting tidbits of conversations, especially dialogue that makes you laugh or cry or get angry. Write descriptions of sunsets. Or traffic accidents. Or sales clerks. Or anything else that catches your attention. Record your reactions to movies. Also write down advice or insights you overhear or someone gives you directly.

90. If you read something that you really like, such as a book, magazine article, newspaper article, or movie review, remember the author's name.

•Check the library for more material by the author, or watch for more articles and stories with the author's byline. Collect as many examples of the author's writing as you can find.

•Read your author's material over and over again. Copy it word for word. Study and analyze the author's style: How long are his or her sentences? Does he or she use familiar words or unfamiliar words? Does she or he use dialogue? Or give detailed descriptions of people or places or action?

•Practice writing the way your favorite author writes. As you get more confident, add your own style, ideas, perspective, and experience.

91. Start working on research papers early so that you have plenty of time for research and thinking.

•There are lots of books available to help you write better book reports and term papers. Go to the library and check them out!

92. When writing a paper, think carefully about how to organize it. Do a detailed outline before you write.

93. Ask a parent or your mentor to read over your papers and give you suggestions.

94. Take your parent's or mentor's feedback seriously. But only if it makes sense to you, too. If it doesn't, ask for an explanation!

95. Always allow time to proofread, correct, and revise your papers before you submit them.

SAMPLE CHECKLIST FOR COMPONENTS OF A TERM PAPER	
	Title Page
	Table of Contents
	Text of Paper
	Footnote Page
	Bibliography or Reference List
	Tables or Figures
	Report Cover or Folder

CHAPTER 10

And Don't Forget

96. Don't cut classes!

97. Do all the schoolwork that is assigned!

98. Pay attention!

99. Ask for help!

100. Don't give up!

101. Whenever you get a chance—**LAUGH!**

Resource Sheets

STEPS IN STUDYING FOR A TEST

1. Choose a study spot.

2. Collect all the books, previous tests, and other materials you will need and bring them to your study spot.

3. Allocate several blocks of study time over a period of several days. DON'T try to "cram" all of your studying into the 24 hours just before the test!

4. Look over old tests and class notes and try to predict the form of the test questions. For example:
- essay
- short answer
- multiple choice
- fill in the blank
- true/false

5. Review the assigned readings and your class notes and try to predict the content of the test questions. Look for the following clues to important material:
- emphasis by the teacher
- subheadings, margin notes, and italics in your textbook

6. Study, study, study!

•Emphasize important content
•Be sure that you fully understand all concepts
•Make a list of difficult concepts, definitions, and proce-
dures for extra study and last minute review

7. Test yourself or ask a parent/mentor/friend to test you.
Mark the items you miss for additional study.

8. Review your list of particularly important and particularly
difficult material.

9. Get a GOOD night's sleep.

10. Eat a GOOD (nutritious) breakfast.

11. Do one more *quick* review of your list.

12. Take the test. STAY CALM no matter what.
•Carefully read each item
•Plan your time
•Think about your answers
•Check your work

BOOK REPORT OUTLINE
FICTION

I. Introduction
   A. Title of book
   B. Author
   C. Publication date
   D. Publisher
   E. Type of book (For example, mystery, science fiction, adventure.)

II. Setting
   A. Time period
   B. Location
   C. Description

III. Characters (Names and Descriptions)
   A. Main character
   B. Other important characters

IV. Summary of the Plot
   A. Problem/situation
   B. Important events
   C. Outcome

V. Critique
   A. Interest level
   B. Quality of writing
   C. What I liked best
   D. What I liked least
   E. Overall opinion of the book

 74

BOOK REPORT OUTLINE
NONFICTION—BIOGRAPHY

I. Introduction
   A. Title of book
   B. Author
   C. Publication date
   D. Publisher
   E. Type of biography (biography or autobiography)

II. Setting
   A. Time period
   B. Location
   C. Description

III. Characters (Names and Descriptions)
   A. Main character
   B. Other important characters

IV. Summary
   A. Background of the person
   B. Important events in the person's life
   C. Obstacles the person overcame
   D. Achievements/insights/values

V. Critique
   A. Interest level
   B. Quality of writing
   C. Best qualities of person
   D. Limitations of person
   E. Important/lasting contributions of person
   F. Overall opinion of the book

ORGANIZING AND WRITING A TERM PAPER
Essential Steps

IMMEDIATELY (as soon as you receive the assignment)

1. Read, reread, and list ALL important parts of the assignment.

2. Question your teacher about any part of the assignment that you do not fully understand.

3. Choose a topic.

4. Ask your teacher to approve your topic.

5. Ask your teacher to suggest any key resources that you should be sure to include as you investigate your topic.

6. Write the due date for the assignment on your planning calendar and allocate ample blocks of time to work on your paper.

AT LEAST THREE WEEKS BEFORE THE TERM PAPER IS DUE

1. Go to the library and browse through any information you can find that is relevant to your topic. Ask the librarian to help you so that you can get a general overview of the scope and availability of information on your topic.

2. Make a checklist of all resources that you will need to obtain and read including:
   •books
   •community resources, such as people to interview or agencies to contact
   •letters to national resources, such as an embassy or organization or club or branch of government
   •phone calls to local resources

3. Obtain all of the resources on your checklist.

4. READ! READ! READ!

5. Take notes on notecards and flag relevant quotes in books and resource materials.

6. CAUTION! Be sure to record accurate and complete reference information as you take notes so that it will be at your fingertips when the time comes to do footnotes and the bibliography.

AT LEAST ONE WEEK BEFORE THE
TERM PAPER IS DUE

1. Review the assignment and make a checklist of all required components of the term paper.

2. Review your notes and THINK about the best way to organize your paper.

3. Do a detailed outline to guide your writing.

4. Write a rough draft.

5. Read and revise your rough draft.

6. Write your final draft.

7. Proofread and correct your final draft.

8. Make sure that you have included all the components on your checklist.

9. Make sure your paper looks good. APPEARANCE COUNTS!

10. Submit your paper ON TIME!

Reference Material

STANDARD WEIGHTS AND MEASURES

There are two measurement systems. The metric system, or the International System, is used in most of the world. The U.S. customary system is used in the United States. The United States is gradually converting to the metric system, but for now, it is important to be familiar with both systems.

Length or Distance
U.S. Customary

1 foot = 12 inches
1 yard = 36 inches = 3 feet
1 mile = 5,280 feet = 1,760 yards

Metric and U.S. Equivalents

1 inch = 2.54 cm or 0.0254 m
1 foot = 30.48 cm or 0.3048 m
1 yard = 91.44 cm or 0.9144 m
1 mile = 1,609.344 m or 1.609344 km
1 m = 39.37 inches
1 km = 0.621 mile

Area
U.S. Customary

1 square foot = 144 square inches
1 square yard = 9 square feet
1 acre = 4,840 square yards or 43,560 square feet
1 square mile = 640 acres

Metric and U.S. Equivalents

1 square foot = 929.030 square cm
1 square yard = 0.836 m
1 acre = 0.405 hectare
1 square mile = 258.999 hectares

Capacities or Volumes
U.S. Customary

1 tablespoon = 3 teaspoons or 0.5 fluid ounce
1 cup = 8 fluid ounces
1 pint = 2 cups or 16 fluid ounces
1 quart = 2 pints or 4 cups or 32 fluid ounces
1 gallon = 4 quarts or 8 pints or 16 cups or 128 fluid ounces
1 bushel = 8 gallons or 32 quarts
1 pound = 16 ounces
1 ton = 2,000 pounds

Metric and U.S. Equivalents

1 cup = 236.588 ml or 0.236588 l
1 pint = 473.176 ml or 0.473176 l
1 quart = 946.3529 ml or 0.9463529 l
1 gallon = 3,758.41 ml or 3.78541 l
1 bushel = 35.238 l

Other Measurements

Bale of cotton: In the U.S., a bale of cotton weighs approximately 500 pounds.

Bolt: Used for measuring cloth, a bolt equals 40 yards.

Cubit: 18 inches or 45.72 cm. Based on the distance between the elbow and the tip of the middle finger.

Hand: 4 inches or 10.16 cm. Used for measuring the height of horses at their withers or the ridge between the horse's shoulder bones.

Karat: Used for measuring the purity of gold, the karat tells how many parts out of 24 are pure.

Knot: Used to measure the speed of ships, the knot is the rate of speed of one nautical mile per hour.

Light-year: 5,880,000,000,000 miles.

BASIC FACTS ABOUT THE UNITED STATES

•Has 50 states

•Alaska is the largest state and Rhode Island is the smallest

•The official 2-letter postal abbreviations for the states are:

Alabama	AL	Kentucky	KY	Ohio	OH
Alaska	AK	Louisiana	LA	Oklahoma	OK
Arizona	AZ	Maine	ME	Oregon	OR
Arkansas	AR	Maryland	MD	Pennsylvania	PA
California	CA	Massachusetts	MA	Rhode Island	RI
Colorado	CO	Michigan	MI	South Carolina	SC
Connecticut	CT	Minnesota	MN	South Dakota	SD
Delaware	DE	Mississippi	MS	Tennessee	TN
Florida	FL	Missouri	MO	Texas	TX
Georgia	GA	Montana	MT	Utah	UT
Hawaii	HI	Nebraska	NE	Vermont	VT
Idaho	ID	Nevada	NV	Virginia	VA
Illinois	IL	New Hampshire	NH	Washington	WA
Indiana	IN	New Jersey	NJ	West Virginia	WV
Iowa	IA	New Mexico	NM	Wisconsin	WI
Kansas	KS	New York	NY	Wyoming	WY
		North Carolina	NC		
		North Dakota	ND		

•Total land area is 3,618,770 square miles

•The United States is the fourth largest country in the world. Only Russia, Canada, and China are larger

•In January 1992 the total U.S. population was estimated at 254,105,000

•There are approximately seven million more women than men in the U.S.

•According to the 1990 census, 80.3% of the population is White (this figure includes Hispanics), 12.1% is Black, 0.8% is Native American (including Eskimos and Aleuts), 2.9% is Asian/Pacific Islander, and 3.9% belong to other races

COMMONLY MISSPELLED WORDS

absence
accessible
accidentally
accommodate
achieve
achievement
actually
address
adolescence
advice
advise
adviser
affect
a lot
all right
almost
already
altogether
argue
arguing
argument
ascend
assassinate
athlete
athletic
awful

balloon
basically
believe
belief
breath
breathe
brilliant
business
cafeteria
calendar
carry
cemetery
chief
choose
choosing
chose
coming
complement
compliment
conceivable
conceive
conscience
criticize
deceive
definite
desert

dessert
dilemma
disastrous
drunkenness
easily
ecstasy
embarrassed
equipped
exceed
exercise
familiar
fascinate
fourth
friend
fulfill
gauge
generally
government
grammar
grateful
grievous
harass
height
heroes
hideous
humorous
identity
imaginary

immigrant
incidentally
interfere
irritable
judgment
kindergarten
later
latter
leisure
library
lightning
likelihood
loneliness
loose
lose
losing
lying
manageable
maneuver
mischief
misspelled
mysterious
necessary
neither
niece
ninety
noticeable
nuisance

obstacle
occasion
occasionally
occur
occurred
original
parallel
pastime
peaceable
permanent
playwright
poison
possession
precede
prejudice
principal
principle
prophecy
psychology
pursue
quiet
quiz
realize
recede
receipt
recommend
reminisce
rhythm

rhythmical
ridiculous
roommate
sacrifice
safety
seize
separate
shepherd
sheriff
similar
similarity
stationary
stationery
strength
strenuous
superintendent
syllable
temperament
temperature
than
their
there
therefore
thorough
through
twelfth
unconscious
unnecessary

unusual
vacuum
versatile
vicious
weather
weird
whether
wholly
written
zigzagged

COMMONLY MISSPELLED PLURALS

arches
beliefs
buzzes
chiefs
cities
echoes
halves
leaves
pianos
potatoes
radios
roofs
tomatoes
zeros

WATCH OUT WHEN YOU USE THESE WORDS

a, an
Use *a* before a word that starts with a consonant (every letter except a, e, i, o, u, and sometimes y). Use *an* before a word that starts with a vowel.

A smart student stays out of food fights.
An eager student does better in school.

affect, effect
Affect means to change or influence something. It can also mean to pretend to feel. *Effect* means to accomplish something. It can also mean the result or impact of something.

The student's decision to do better in school *affected* her performance.
When the teacher postponed the test, the student *affected* disappointment.
With ease, the well-prepared student *effected* an outstanding oral report.
The student's appeal for more time to complete the homework assignment because of a hurt toe had no *effect* on the teacher.

all ready, already
Use *all ready* when you mean all of the things or people. Use *already* to mean "by this or that time."

90

When they saw the cafeteria food, the students were *all ready* to eat grass and bugs.

The teacher quickly turned around, but the students had *already* stopped making spitballs.

bad, badly

Use *bad* when you mean "not good," "sick," or "sorry." Use *badly* when you mean "not well." When used with "want" or "need," *badly* means "very much."

The student ate nine sugared donuts for lunch and felt *bad* for the rest of the day.

The student didn't study for a test and did *badly*.

When it started snowing, the students *badly* wanted school to be canceled.

capital, capitol

Use *capital* when you mean the seat of government, or punishment by death, or accumulated wealth. *Capital* also means the type of letter at the beginning of a sentence or the first letter of a name. Use *capitol* when you mean the building in which the state or federal legislatures meet.

Trenton is the *capital* of New Jersey.

Murder is a *capital* crime in some states.

Capital includes money, real estate, stocks, and bonds.

Michelle starts with a *capital* "M" whether it is at the beginning or end of a sentence.

The House of Representatives and the Senate meet in the United States *Capitol* Building in Washington, DC.

envelop, envelope
Use *envelop* when you mean "cover" or "enclose." Use *envelope* when you mean the container for storing or mailing letters and papers.

Dust seemed to *envelop* the horses as they galloped around the dirt track.

He put the love letter in a blue *envelope* and sealed it with a wet kiss.

Bibliography

Berry, Marilyn. *Help is on the Way for: Study Habits.* Chicago: Childrens Press, 1985.
Other books by Marilyn Berry include:
- *Help is on the Way for: Tests*
- *Help is on the Way for: Book Reports*

Bounds, Sarah. *Food for Health and Vitality.* London: Ward Lock Ltd., 1985.

Ewald, Ellen Buchman. *Recipes for a Small Planet.* New York: Ballantine Books, 1973.

Ferraro, Susan. *Remembrance of Things Fast.* New York: Dell Publishing, 1990.

Fleisher, Paul. *Changing Our World: A Handbook for Young Activists.* Tucson, Arizona: Zephyr Press, 1993.

Fry, Ron. *How To Study.* Hawthorne, New Jersey: Career Press, 1991.
Other books by Ron Fry include:
- *Take Notes*
- *Improve Your Reading*
- *Write Papers*
- *Manage Your Time*

James, Elizabeth and Carol Barkin. *How To Be School Smart.* New York: Beech Tree Books, 1988.
Other books by Elizabeth James and Carol Barkin include:
- *How to Write A Great School Report*
- *How to Write Your Best Book Report*
- *How to Write A Term Paper*

Rafoth, Mary Ann and Leonard DeFabo. *Study Skills*.
    Washington, D.C. National Education Association, 1992.
Scott, Sharon. *PPR: Peer Pressure Reversal—How to Say No
    and Keep Your Friends*. Amherst, Massachusetts:
    Human Resource Development Press, 1986.